Advanced Piano

Popular PERFORMER

Great American Songbook BOOK 3

Arranged by DAN COATES

The Best Hits from Timeless Songwriters

The Great American Songbook contains the best popular music ever written. This volume revisits some of those songs, casting them in the rich voice of the piano. Standards by legendary songwriters are included: "Love Is Here to Stay" by George and Ira Gershwin, "Where or When" by Richard Rodgers and Lorenz Hart, "Skylark" by Hoagy Carmichael, and "I've Got You Under My Skin" by Cole Porter. The bluesy chords of "Cry Me a River," the confident stride of "It Had to Be You," and all of the other wonderful musical moments are certain to provide hours of enjoyment for the pianist who wishes to be a *Popular Performer*.

CONTENTS

GERSHWIN®, GEORGE GERSHWIN® and IRA GERSHWIN™
are registered trademarks of Gershwin Enterprises

Produced by
Alfred Music
P.O. Box 10003
Van Nuys, CA 91410-0003
alfred.com

Printed in USA.

ISBN-10: 0-7390-9664-8
ISBN-13: 978-0-7390-9664-2

CRY ME A RIVER

Words and Music by Arthur Hamilton
Arr. Dan Coates

I Only Have Eyes for You

Words by Al Dubin
Music by Harry Warren
Arr. Dan Coates

Moderately slow, with expression (♩ = 96)

I'm in the Mood for Love

Words and Music by
Jimmy McHugh and Dorothy Fields
Arr. Dan Coates

I'VE GOT YOU UNDER MY SKIN

Words and Music by Cole Porter
Arr. Dan Coates

14

It Had to Be You

Words by Gus Kahn
Music by Isham Jones
Arr. Dan Coates

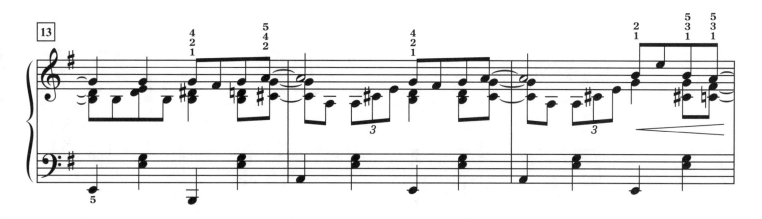

LOVE IS HERE TO STAY

Music and Lyrics by
George Gershwin and Ira Gershwin
Arr. Dan Coates

Make Someone Happy

Lyrics by Betty Comden and Adolph Green
Music by Jule Styne
Arr. Dan Coates

SKYLARK

Words by Johnny Mercer
Music by Hoagy Carmichael
Arr. Dan Coates

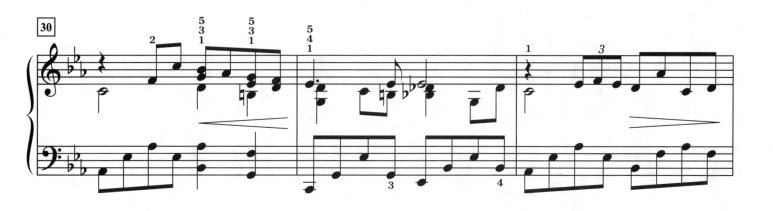

SUMMERTIME

Music and Lyrics by George Gershwin,
DuBose and Dorothy Heyward and Ira Gershwin
Arr. Dan Coates

Moderately slow, with expression ($\quarternote = 72$)

WHERE OR WHEN

Words by Lorenz Hart
Music by Richard Rodgers
Arr. Dan Coates

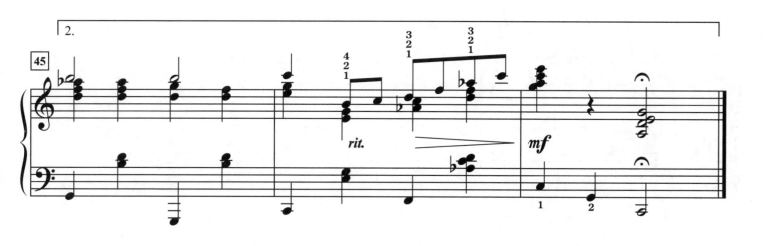

WHAT A WONDERFUL WORLD

Words and Music by
George David Weiss and Bob Thiele
Arr. Dan Coates

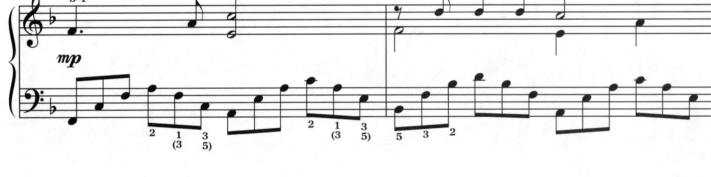

YOU'LL NEVER KNOW

Lyrics by Mack Gordon
Music by Harry Warren
Arr. Dan Coates

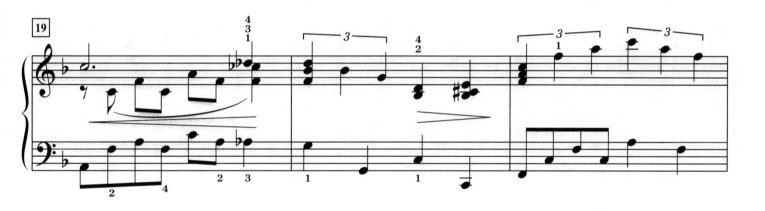